Staying Safe

www.SteckVaughn.com
800-531-5015

Staying Safe

contents

Staying Safe
Fact Matters

ISBN-13: 978-1-4190-5472-3
ISBN-10: 1-4190-5472-4

First published by Blake Education Pty Ltd as *Go Facts*
Copyright © 2006 Blake Publishing
This edition copyright under license from Blake Education Pty Ltd
© 2010 Steck-Vaughn, an imprint of HMH Supplemental Publishers Inc.

Printed in China

1 2 3 4 5 6 7 8   373   15 14 13 12 11 10 09 08

What Is Safety?

*Every environment has possible **hazards**. By being **conscious** of the hazards, it is often possible to avoid danger and harm.*

People make decisions every day that keep them safe. Most people naturally check for traffic before crossing a road. They also generally keep away from the edge of a cliff.

Sometimes you have to think more carefully about possible hazards. For example, camping can be a dangerous activity if you aren't prepared for the weather. Most campers watch the weather forecasts for days or weeks ahead of time. That way they will know what kind of gear and clothing to bring. They will also know if it's safer to stay home.

Your body gives warning signals when there is danger. Your palms sweat. Your heart beats faster. Keeping calm can **minimize risk**.

First to the Rescue

First aid is immediate treatment for someone who is ill or injured. It happens before a doctor has the chance to help. Anyone can learn first aid for treating minor injuries. Minor injuries include cuts, sprains, and stings.

The term **medevac** stands for "medical evacuation." It generally refers to the use of helicopters to get seriously injured patients to hospitals as quickly as possible.

Did You Know?

On average, about 700 people die in the United States every year from heat-related causes.

Campers must carry all of their safety equipment with them.

A first aid kit should include bandages, scissors, **antiseptic**, and basic medicines.

Lifeguards are trained in rescue techniques and first aid.

CAUTION
Wet Floor

Cuidado
Piso Mojado

Signs warn people of hazards.

Road Safety

On average, 118 people are killed every day on roads in the United States.

Cars Can Kill

Being a safe **pedestrian** means being visible and crossing roads at the safest locations. Safe locations include at traffic lights, at pedestrian crossings, and away from parked cars.

Inside a car, seat belts and air bags save lives. Drivers and passengers who don't wear a seat belt are 18 times more likely to be killed in a road accident than those wearing a seat belt. In 1984, New York was the first state to pass a law making it **compulsory** for all passengers to wear a seat belt.

On Your Bike

On the road, bicycles are considered vehicles. Cyclists have a right to use the road. However, they must obey all road rules.

Some roads have lanes for cyclists. Bike lanes reduce the chance of accidents between cars and bicycles, especially on busy city streets.

Cyclists can be difficult to see. They should wear bright or light-colored clothing. They should ride a few feet away from the gutter and parked cars. Cyclists should constantly scan the environment for pedestrians and other vehicles.

Bicycle helmets save lives and reduce the risk of head injuries. Helmets have a foam shell that absorbs much of the impact to the head during an accident.

Did You Know?

The main cause of injury and death in a car crash is the driver and passengers being thrown around inside the car. At 30 miles per hour, the impact is like falling from the top of a three-story building. Seat belts stop this danger and reduce the risk of injury and death.

About 80 percent of cyclists admitted to hospitals did not collide with another vehicle. They lost control of their bicycles.

When riding with friends, each rider should know the laws and follow road safety.

Air bags cut the chance of getting a serious head injury in an accident in half.

More than half the injuries that cause death for 10–14-year-olds are due to road accidents.

Burns

*Burns damage the surface of the skin. They may also damage deep tissues. Severe burns can lead to **shock**, infection, and death.*

Types of Burns

There are three types of burn injuries.

First-Degree Burn

The epidermis, or outer layer of skin, is burned. These burns heal well after being cooled with water.

Second-Degree Burn

The epidermis is burned and it blisters. These burns need medical treatment.

Third-Degree Burn

All layers of the skin are burned. Nerves, tissues, and muscles are damaged. These burns need emergency medical treatment.

The deeper the burn and the greater the body area it covers, the greater the risk to the patient. Burnt airways can make breathing difficult.

Treating Burns

It is important to treat all burns quickly to reduce pain and prevent scarring. Treatment aims to stop the burning, relieve pain and swelling, and minimize the risk of infection.

First Aid for a Burn:

1. Run cool water over the burn.
2. Remove any jewelry, belts, or tight clothing near the burn.
3. Cover the burn with a clean towel or bandage.
4. Decide whether additional treatment is needed.

If the body cannot heal a burn itself, doctors may repair the burn with a skin graft. Healthy skin is taken from an area that is usually covered, such as the thigh. The skin is laid over the wound and stitched or stapled into position.

A bad sunburn can be a second-degree burn.

It takes five minutes for water at 120 degrees Fahrenheit to cause a first-degree burn. It takes just one second for water at 140 degrees Fahrenheit to cause the same burn.

Deep burns may not be as painful as surface burns because the deep burns destroy nerve endings.

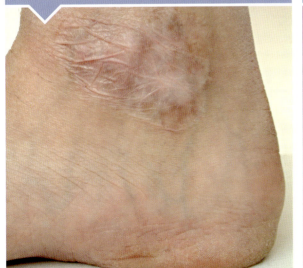

Smoke alarms provide an early warning of a home fire.

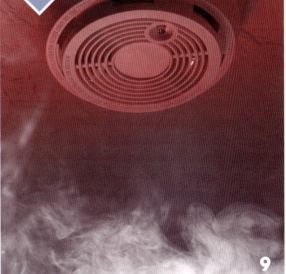

Poisoning and Bites

Poisons are substances that enter the bloodstream and cause illness or death. Venoms are poisons produced by animals.

Poison

Many household products, such as medicines, pesticides, and cleaning supplies, are poisonous. Young children are most at risk from poisoning. Poisonous products should be locked out of reach and sight.

The symptoms of poisoning depend on the poison and how much is swallowed. Symptoms may include vomiting, stomach pain, and drowsiness.

The bluebottle, or Portuguese man-of-war, delivers a painful sting even if it is dead.

Bites and Stings

About 8,000 people are bitten by snakes every year in the United States. Most venomous snakes live in the southern or southeastern parts of the country.

Most bites can be avoided by simply leaving snakes alone. Wear thick shoes or boots that cover the ankles. Never put hands into places where snakes may hide, like in hollow logs.

To treat a snakebite in the past, the venom was sucked out of the victim. Whoever sucked out the venom then vomited. This often caused more damage than the bite! The correct treatment for a snakebite is to wrap a bandage a few inches from the bite, between the bite and the heart. The victim should stay very still to keep the venom from moving through the body.

Are these pills or candy?* Many medicines look like candy or chewing gum. They should always be kept out of children's reach.

*They are pills.

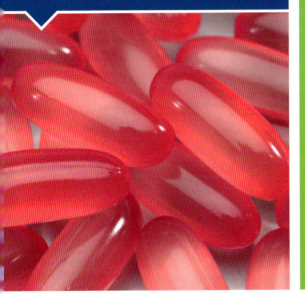

A male platypus has venomous spurs on the back of its legs. Pain from an attack can last for days or weeks.

The Australian funnel-web spider is one of the most dangerous spiders in the world. Its fangs are large and powerful enough to puncture a fingernail. Antivenin, a drug that cancels the effect of venom, has been available for this species since 1980. Since then, there have been no recorded deaths from this spider's bite.

It's an Emergency!

An ambulance service provides care at the scene of a medical emergency and on the way to the hospital.

Calling for Help

Dial 911 to contact emergency services. This call is free from any phone.

Try to stay calm and speak slowly. An operator will ask you several questions, which include:

- What is the exact location of the emergency?
- What is the phone number you're calling from?
- What is the problem? Tell me exactly what happened.

Help on the Way

The operator decides how **urgent** the emergency is based on your answers. He or she contacts the police and, if necessary, an ambulance. The operator will also tell the **paramedics** the details of the emergency.

While help is on the way, it is important for you to stay on the phone. The operator may have instructions or more questions.

When the ambulance arrives, the paramedics will **assess** the situation. They will take over any treatment that has begun. If necessary, they will take the person to a hospital.

Ambulance is often printed backward on the front of the vehicle. This is so a driver in front can read it correctly through a rearview mirror—and then get out of the way!

Lights and sirens are used only if the patient's condition is life-threatening or quickly getting worse.

An air ambulance is used to transport extremely ill or injured patients and to reach emergencies in remote areas.

Paramedics usually work in pairs.

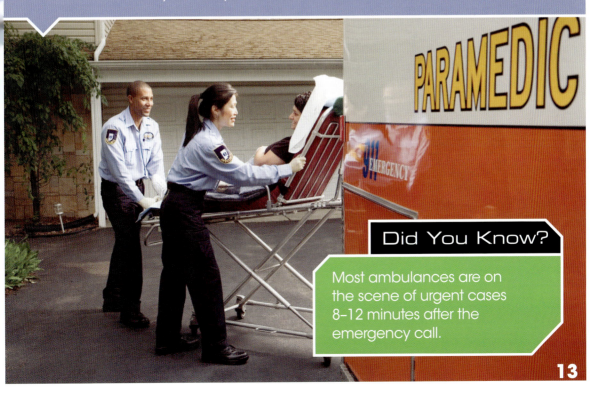

Did You Know?

Most ambulances are on the scene of urgent cases 8–12 minutes after the emergency call.

Electrical Shock

*The human body is a good **conductor** of electricity.*

Electricity rushes through the body during an electrical shock. It burns the skin and internal tissues. The burns are worst where the electricity enters and leaves the body. Electricity can also make the heart beat unevenly or stop.

Electrical shock can occur from touching power lines, faulty appliances, or damaged cords. It is also caused by lightning and by touching electrical appliances that are near water.

To use electricity safely, check that plugs and cords are in good condition. Do not use anything electrical near water, such as around a bathtub or pool. Never touch anything electrical with wet hands.

A licensed electrician should do all electrical work around the house. A safety switch between a power point and an appliance can **detect** if the appliance is faulty. If an electrical shock is about to occur, the switch shuts down electricity in 1/30,000 of a second.

Treating a Shock

If you are with someone who receives an electrical shock, act quickly. Turn off the power supply. Do not touch the person until the power supply is turned off. Start **resuscitation** if the person has stopped breathing. Dial 911 for an ambulance.

Never overload a plug.

Electricians use fiberglass or wooden ladders. Metal ladders conduct electricity.

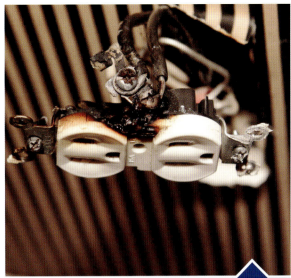

Old electrical wiring and switches can be dangerous. An electrical fault melted this plug. This fault could have started a fire.

Indoors is the safest place to be during an electrical storm.

Did You Know?

Ex-park ranger Roy C. Sullivan was struck by lightning seven times and survived.

Body Fluids

Blood and other body fluids can carry disease. People can become infected if they don't handle body fluids safely.

Body fluids include blood, saliva, and urine. These fluids can carry deadly viruses and bacterial infections.

A person can pass a disease to another person if body fluids get into the mouth, eyes, or open cuts. Diseases can also be passed on by **contaminated** equipment and unclean work areas.

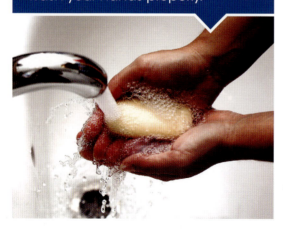

It takes at least 20 seconds to wash your hands properly.

At Risk

Some people are at risk of infection from body fluids because of the work they do. Doctors, nurses, and research scientists handle body fluids every day. They wear masks, glasses, and gloves for protection. They may also be **vaccinated** against dangerous viruses.

They always wash their hands with soap and water before and after examining a patient. They also wash after handling body fluids. Disposable needles are used only once.

In most contact sports, if an injured player is bleeding, he or she must leave the game until the bleeding stops. This rule allows the injured player to be treated. It also protects other players from contact with blood.

Paramedics always wear gloves when they treat an injured person.

Some research procedures are done inside a biocabinet to prevent splashing or infection.

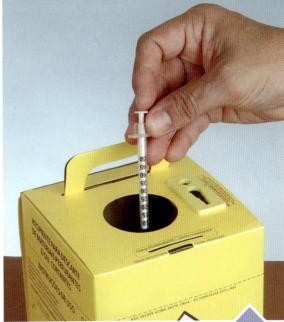

Needles and blades that have touched body fluids are put in special trash containers.

What Is Shock?

What does it mean when somebody "goes into shock"?

The human body needs oxygen. Blood carries oxygen to all the body's organs. The body goes into shock if it is not getting enough blood.

Many factors can cause shock. Heart attacks and sudden and massive blood loss can stop blood from reaching organs.

Symptoms of Shock

In the early stages of shock, the patient's heart rate quickens. The skin becomes cold and clammy. It may become pale blue-gray, especially around the lips.

Breathing becomes rapid and shallow. The patient may feel weak and dizzy. Other symptoms include **nausea**, thirst, and a weak pulse.

Severe shock may lead to **unconsciousness** and death.

Dangerous Allergies

A special type of shock is called anaphylactic shock. It is a severe allergic reaction, usually to peanuts, seafood, insect stings, or medicines.

Symptoms include difficulty breathing and talking. This difficulty is caused by swelling in the throat. Young children become pale and weak.

Anaphylactic shock needs urgent medical attention because it can kill in seconds. The emergency treatment is an injection of adrenaline. Adrenaline is a chemical produced by the body that makes the heart beat faster. People who know they are allergic to certain foods often carry adrenaline with them.

Did You Know?

More than 12 million Americans have food allergies.

A skin allergy test can detect a food allergy. The skin is poked with a needle. Then a drop of **allergen** is placed on the skin. If a person is allergic, a small bump like a mosquito bite appears.

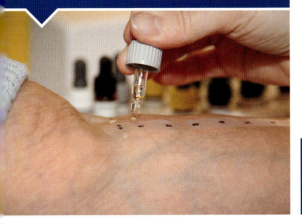

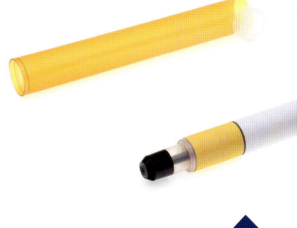

This device gives an automatic injection of adrenaline when jabbed into the thigh.

People donate blood to be used by someone needing a transfusion.

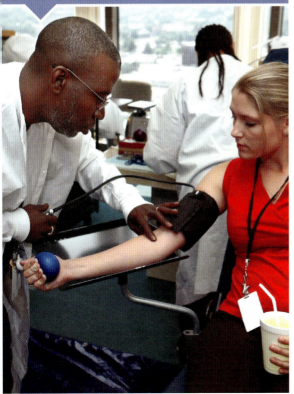

Many schools ban nuts and peanut butter to protect children who have food allergies.

Survival Swimming

All swimming places—pools, rivers, lakes, and the ocean—have hazards. Survival swimming is a group of skills to help survive an emergency in the water.

Survival swimming includes the ability to swim and stay afloat while fully dressed.

Check for Hazards

Many people are seriously injured jumping or diving into water that is too shallow. Check out any swimming spot before jumping or diving in. Do this by getting into the water to check the depth. Also, make sure that the area is clear of rocks, roots, sandbanks, and weeds.

Did You Know?

Every year nearly 71,000 people are rescued in the U.S. by trained lifeguards.

Rip Currents

A **rip current** is a strong ocean current heading away from shore. It can flow as fast as six miles per hour and drag swimmers more than 1,000 feet offshore. People often try to swim against the rip. They often become exhausted and drown. About 80 percent of beach rescues are for people caught in rip currents.

Remember the three R's if you are caught in a rip current:

- RELAX—float or swim with the current, not against it.
- RAISE—lift one arm to signal for help.
- RESCUE—float and wait for help.

Before going boating, check the weather conditions.
While boating, always wear a personal flotation device.

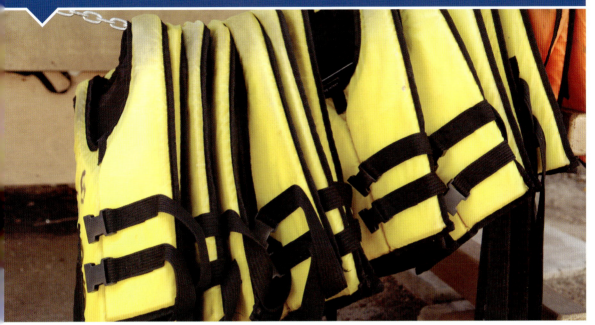

If there is a boating accident, stay with the boat. Hold onto any floating objects and huddle with other people.

Always check safety signs before entering the water.

The brain can survive for only three to four minutes without the blood's oxygen. Resuscitation restores breathing and gets the heart pumping again.

The ABCs of resuscitation describe how an unconscious person can be helped.

A is for Airway

Open the airway by tilting the head gently back. Look for blockages. Watch the chest to see if it rises and falls. Listen for breathing sounds.

B is for Breathing

If the patient is not breathing, start mouth-to-mouth resuscitation. Also called rescue breathing, this procedure involves breathing air into the person's lungs.

C is for Circulation

Check for a pulse. The easiest place to check is on the neck, below the person's jawbone. If there is no pulse, **cardiopulmonary resuscitation** (CPR) is started. CPR combines rescue breathing with pushes on the chest. The pushes massage the heart and keep oxygenated blood flowing to the brain and other organs.

Learn to Save

Resuscitation is a valuable skill. First aid courses teach people how to resuscitate someone safely. If not performed properly, CPR can cause broken ribs and damaged lungs. NEVER practice on a person who does not need it!

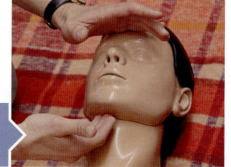

People use dummies to practice resuscitation.

CPR saves more lives on television and in the movies than it does in real life.

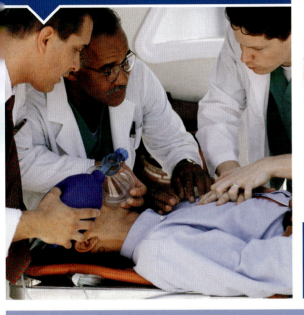

Exhaled air contains about 15 percent oxygen. That is enough to help an unconscious person.

Did You Know?

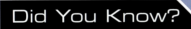

The heart pumps more than 66 million gallons of blood in an average lifetime.

Paramedics often use a BVM (bag-valve-mask) for rescue breathing. It can also be connected to an oxygen supply.

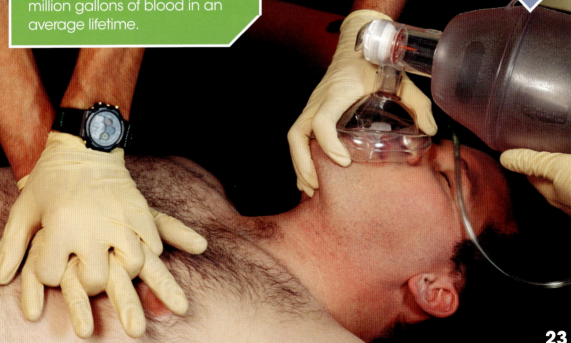

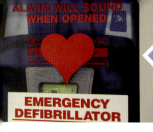
Heart Starters

*Emergency workers may use a **defibrillator** to make a heart pump blood.*

In a **cardiac arrest,** the heart stops pumping blood. A cardiac arrest is also known as a heart attack. It may happen because of heart disease, electric shock, or severe blood loss. Sometimes the heart quivers like jelly after a cardiac arrest rather than lying still. The heart's muscle fibers are contracting, but not in a regular way. The heart cannot pump blood this way.

Paddles

A defibrillator is a machine designed to make the heart beat normally. It has metal paddles, or **electrodes**, that are held against the skin near the patient's heart.

The defibrillator gives an electrical shock to the heart. Electricity passes from one paddle, through the heart, and out the other paddle.

The shock stops the action of individual muscle fibers. It allows a normal heartbeat to start beating again.

Automatic Version

Many ambulances carry a defibrillator. All hospital emergency wards have them. An automatic defibrillator monitors a heart's rhythm. It automatically delivers an electric shock if required. People who are at risk of having a cardiac arrest may have a small, battery-powered defibrillator **implanted** in their chests.

Did You Know?

Defibrillation can improve a patient's chance of survival to well over 50 percent if used within three minutes of a cardiac arrest.

The paddles are insulated to protect the user from electrical shock.

Most cardiac arrests occur away from hospitals. Automated defibrillators are installed in many public places.

In a hospital, a cart that contains a defibrillator and drugs to treat a cardiac arrest is called a crash cart.

A defibrillator's shock lasts only 4–12 milliseconds.

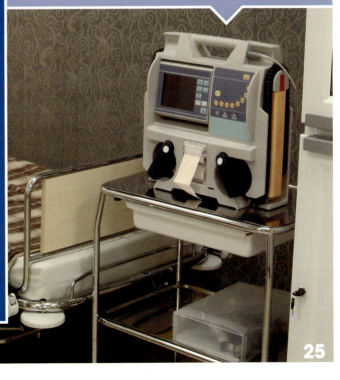

Home Safety Checklist

Most accidents happen around the home. How safe is your home?

Complete this home safety checklist to see how your home rates.

What to Do:

1. Photocopy the table on the opposite page.
2. Check your home, room by room, and answer "Yes" or "No" for each question.
3. Working with an adult, take action to improve safety where needed. Then check under "Action Taken."

	Yes	No	Action Taken
General			
Do you have working smoke alarms?			
Are electrical cords out of sight and reach of children?			
Are all curtain and blind cords out of reach of children?			
Is top-heavy furniture (bookshelves, televisions, etc.) secure and stable?			
Is there a first aid kit in the house?			
Do you have the phone number for Poison Control and other emergency services beside every phone?			
Kitchen			
Is there a fire blanket or fire extinguisher nearby?			
Are cleaning products and knives out of reach?			
Are appliances and cords out of reach?			
Living room			
Are heaters clear of curtains and furniture?			
Are safety covers in unused plugs?			
Are sharp edges of furniture covered?			
Laundry room			
Are cleaning products out of reach and locked away?			
Have old and unused poisonous products been thrown away?			
Bathroom			
Is there a bath mat to prevent slipping?			
Are medicines out of reach and locked away?			
Garage/Shed and Outside			
Are all chemicals (paints, gardening products, etc.) out of reach and locked away?			
If you have a pool or spa, is it surrounded by a 4-foot-high fence with a self-closing and self-latching gate?			
Is there a CPR poster near the pool/spa?			

Staying Safe

Who is responsible for your safety?

When we are children, our parents look after our needs and keep us safe. As we grow up, we become responsible for our actions and our own safety.

It's Your Choice

Peer groups are groups of friends who are all about the same age. They help us become independent.

Pressure from a peer group can sometimes lead us into doing things we would not normally do. Sometimes peers are right. Sometimes they are wrong. The best way to keep safe

is to make your own decisions about your safety. This is also a good way to keep the respect of your friends, family, and self.

Your Safety Situation

You must consider situations and decide how safe they are. Think of a traffic light.

When a traffic light is green, it is safe to go forward. If the light is yellow, you should be careful and prepare to stop. If the light turns red, you must stop.

Use the same idea to know when you are safe, need to use caution, or should stop because there is danger. It is important to teach yourself to recognize different kinds of situations. You must be aware when your safety situation changes from green to yellow or to red.

Parents and teachers can only guide you. You are responsible for yourself and the choices you make.

Did You Know?

Alcohol and other drugs affect a person's ability to make safe decisions. More than one-third of pedestrians killed in the United States every year have a blood alcohol reading higher than the legal limit.

Are You a Safe Cyclist?

Do you know enough to make safe decisions on the road? You'll find the answers to these quiz questions on the index page.

True or False?

1 You must stop at red traffic lights.

2 You may ride beside another cyclist on a road.

3 It's OK to ride through a stop sign if there are no other cars around.

4 It is safe to ride at night without lights as long as you wear reflective clothing.

5 Cyclists of all ages should wear helmets.

6 If you've got good balance, it's OK to ride with no hands on the handlebars.

7 You don't need to use a hand signal if you are turning right.

8 You may carry someone else on your bike if they wear a helmet.

9 You should never listen to music while riding a bike.

10 You can hang on to another vehicle while riding your bike as long as you don't go over the speed limit.

Glossary

allergen (AL uhr juhn) a substance that causes an allergic reaction

antiseptic (AN tuh SEHP tihk) a substance that prevents infection by killing germs

assess (uh SEHS) to judge a situation or object

cardiac arrest (KAHR dee ak uh REHST) the sudden stopping of the heartbeat; heart attack

cardiopulmonary resuscitation (KAHR dee oh PUL muh NEHR ee rih SUHS uh TAY shuhn) the use of chest compressions and breaths to revive someone whose heart has stopped beating

compulsory (kuhm PUHL suhr ee) required by law; mandatory

conductor (kuhn DUHK tuhr) something through which electricity passes easily

conscious (KON shuhs) awake, thinking, and aware

contaminated (kuhn TAM uh nay tihd) spoiled or impure because of contact with something unclean

defibrillator (dee FIH bruh LAY tuhr) a machine that sends an electric shock through a person to stabilize the heartbeat

detect (dih TEHKT) to notice or discover the existence of something

electrodes (ih LEHK trohds) conductors through which electricity enters or leaves something

hazards (HAZ uhrdz) things that could be dangerous

implanted (ihm PLANT tihd) inserted into the body using surgery

medevac (MEHD ih VAK) medical evacuation; using helicopters to transport critically ill or injured patients to hospitals as quickly as possible

minimize (MIHN uh myz) to reduce something as much as possible

nausea (NAW see uh) a feeling that you are going to vomit

paramedics (PAR uh MEHD ihks) people who are trained to do medical work, especially in emergencies, but who are not doctors or nurses

pedestrian (puh DEHS tree uhn) a person who is walking

resuscitation (rih SUHS uh TAY shuhn) techniques used to return someone to life or consciousness

rip current (rihp KUR uhnt) a fast flow of water from shore out to sea

risk (rihsk) the danger or likelihood that something bad will happen

shock (shok) a state in which your body begins to shut down from lack of blood

unconsciousness (uhn KON shuhs nihs) the state of being asleep or otherwise unaware of what is happening

urgent (UR juhnt) needing immediate attention or action

vaccinated (VAK suh nay tihd) to have been given a substance which contains a safe form of a virus or bacterium; to be protected from getting the disease which the virus or bacterium causes

Index

Answers to quiz on page 30
1–true 2–true 3–false 4–false 5–true 6–false
7–false 8–false 9–true 10–false